JEFF SIMPSON

VERTICAL HOLD

STEEL TOE BOOKS
Bowling Green, Kentucky

JEFF SIMPSON

VERTICAL HOLD

ISBN 978-0-9824169-5-2

STEEL TOE BOOKS
Western Kentucky University
Department of English
1906 College Heights Blvd. #11086
Bowling Green, KY 42101-1086
steeltoebooks.com

COVER PHOTOGRAPH
Arnis Balcus

AUTHOR PHOTOGRAPH
Chelsey Simpson

COVER AND BOOK DESIGN
Molly McCaffrey

Early forms of anti-shake technology involved a physical corrector in the shape of an oil-filled bellows-effect prism lens inside the optical block. These artifices have become necessary as camcorders have shrunk in size and weight and been given longer zoom lenses: the human hands that hold them tend to tremble, one of the many physiological factors for which technology has to cater.

–NEWNES TELEVISION AND VIDEO ENGINEER'S POCKET BOOK

Twentieth-century, go to sleep.

–R.E.M.

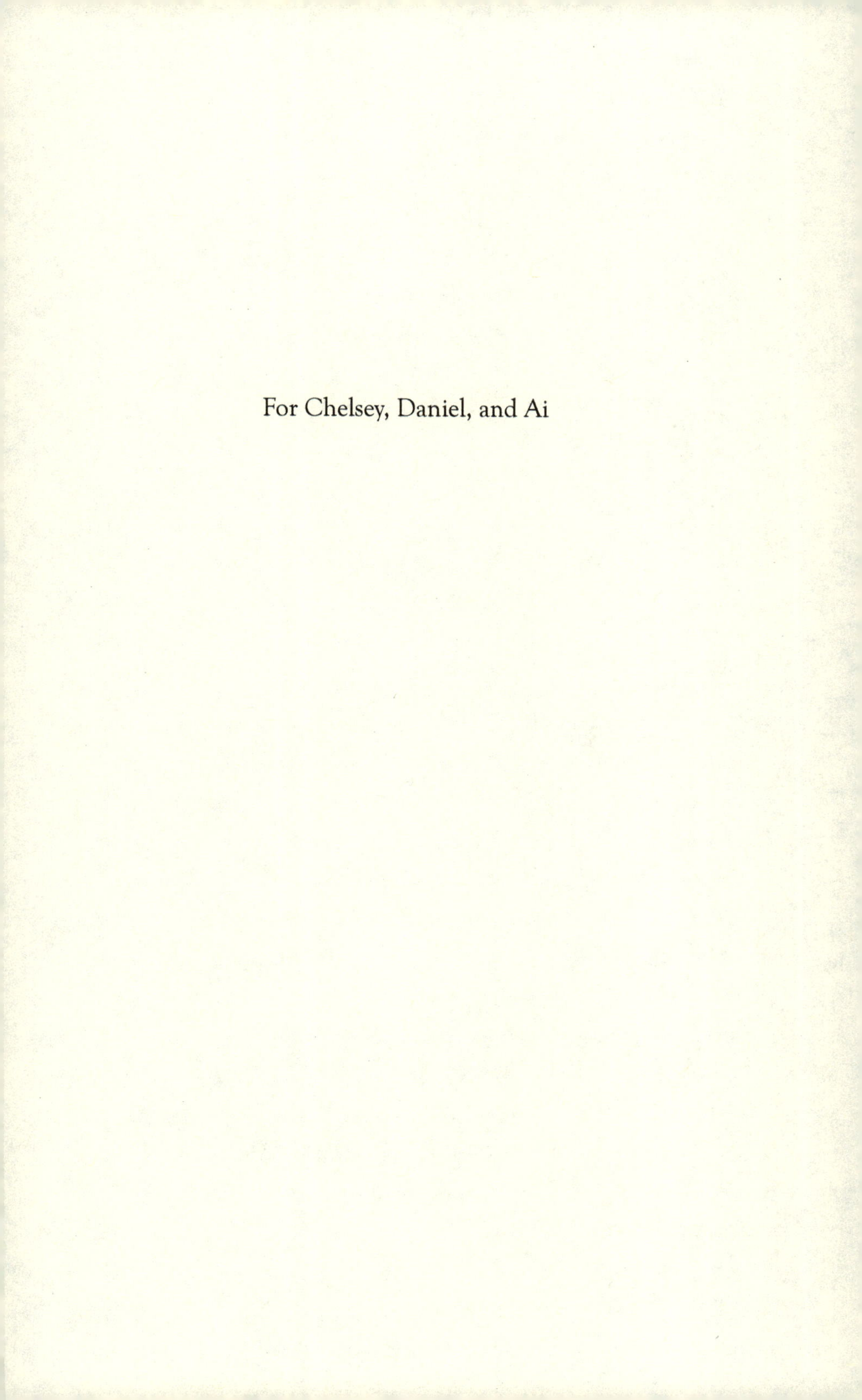

For Chelsey, Daniel, and Ai

CONTENTS

ONE

Lessons in Childhood Development 3
Miami, OK 6
Ode to the Man in Red Sweatpants 8
Swimming the English Channel 10
Ode to Love Handles 12
Letter from a Hypochondriac 14
Upon Reading Elvin Jones has Died of Heart Failure in Englewood, NJ 16
Poem Beginning in the Front Seat of a Cadillac 17
Overtime 19
Song 21
Stag Night 22
Reunions 24
SNAFU 27

TWO

Ode to Suede 37
Thyroidectomy 39
The Fifth of July 41
There Are Worse Things I Could Do 44

Phosphorus 46
Ghost of a Chance 48
B.A. in English 50
October: A Letter 52
Paris, TX 53
Communion 55

THREE

If You Ain't Got the Do Re Mi 61
Letter Sent Via Amniocentesis 65
Phantom Pains 67
Into Soil 69
Hymn 70
Still Life with Pomegranates 72
Color Depicting the Inherent Value of Things 73
Hollow Light 76
Elegy for What Can't be Said 77
Flash Point 79
Feedback Loop for the Apocalypse 80
Shrapnel 84
Elegy with a Balcony and Opening Credits 86

ONE

LESSONS IN CHILDHOOD DEVELOPMENT

If you were breastfed, consider yourself lucky.
You'll have a healthier immune system
and be less likely to develop suicidal tendencies
as an adult. But if you started on the bottle,
you'll always be on the bottle, and life shall be
a downhill scooter race from that point forward.
Early physical objects will play a formative role
and continue to hold immense psychic weight
well into adulthood. Imagine your first bedroom
with the clown wallpaper border. If you favored
the hobo clown with the five o'clock shadow,
knapsack tied neatly to a stick, you'll forever plan
exit strategies and possess a disproportionate love
for songs and movies about the open road.
This will be one of the chief complaints your wife
will dredge up years later during marital counseling.
Other possible items include, but are not limited to:
a Hulk Hogan action figure; autographed Ken Griffey,
Jr. rookie card; gold pocket watch circa 1850;
homemade slingshot; arrowheads; prosthetic hook;
illegal bottle rockets you kept in the closet waiting
for the right moment, which never came, etcetera,
etcetera. Parental relations will be instrumental
in your ability to sustain a marriage into your golden
years. The day your father throws a banana at your mother
you'll realize that even the most harmless things bruise.
The night your mother chases your father with a butcher
knife you'll learn that everything has a certain order
and place—*the flour jar sits next to the sugar jar next*

to the coffee canister. Picture busted cabinet doors,
hinges missing screws, but everything so clean
it's like a museum installment, like a memory
about to break—the saucer and plate.
Physical and psychological trauma are necessary
to prepare yourself for later disappointment,
but there are things to avoid: Don't run across the linoleum
floor with socks on, especially when it shines so bright
you'll swear it's made of glass. Never stage a BB gun
war in your backyard regardless of how much
your teacher discusses the Jewish-Palestinian conflict.
Many shall be wounded. Someone will lose an eye,
someone part of a tooth. In fact, sell your BB guns
to Doug. He's naïve, as is his mom who comes home
from the tire plant so tired and frail she'll let him
get away with anything. When you hit puberty
and feel like a balloon in your stomach is about to pop,
take your frustrations out on something besides
the family pet. If you must, hurt yourself. Thumbtacks
work well, and if you're really having a bad day,
shoot yourself in the hand with a CO_2-powered
BB gun, unless you sold it to Doug, who'll buy
anything—back issues of *Penthouse*,
expired valium. Know that the smell of bacon
and pancakes will always be comforting.
When your wife leaves you in your early 30s
remember to make this meal the next morning.
If it doesn't help, order pigs in a blanket for lunch.
They taste similar but are more acceptable
for noontime consumption. And if you still feel
like a dumpster that's been set on fire for Halloween,

shoot yourself in the hand with a staple gun or drag
a letter opener across your forehead. Tell coworkers
you're suffering from seasonal stigmata and ask
for the rest of the day off. On your way home,
stop by Doug's place. Show him your wedding band,
the pocket watch, the autographed rookie card.
Ask how he's doing. Ask what he'll take.

MIaMI, OK

I can do whatever I want. I'm rich, I'm famous, and I'm bigger than you.
—Don Johnson

My parents' bedroom, 1987, gateway to the land
of Technicolor and remote controls, where every Thursday
that electric opening fueled by stereophonic guitars
and Afro-Caribbean drums would echo through the house,
signaling the beginning of *Miami Vice*—wild flamingos
and busty women, sweeping helicopter shots of the great
Atlantic surf crashing into South Beach. How could you
not love the barely plausible exploits of Crockett & Tubbs
as they operated undercover, driving Ferraris and go-fast boats
and wooing all those cocoa-butter damsels in distress?
How could you not love the slip-on, sockless loafers,
white linen pants, Armani jackets, t-shirts in shades of pink,
blue, green, and fuchsia, the big-ass Ray-Bans and Floridian
sunsets falling behind the buildings of downtown Miami?
My mother loved Don Johnson the way girls once loved
The Beatles or Elvis, and she often joked she'd leave my father
for her Don Juan of the Everglades with his rugged good looks,
tan skin, and slick hair, leaving me and my younger brother
to feel sorry for a Scots-Irish lineman with a cleft chin
and a bad temper. The poor bastard wouldn't stand a chance,
we thought, should fate intercede, and, late at night,
listening to our parents have sex from our twin bunk beds,
giggling at the asthmatic breathing and muffled moans
that sometimes sounded like pain, I'd picture his ghost-image
lingering on the screen, all beard stubble and white teeth,
watching them make love in the dark. How could you blame

her for the fantasy of a glamorous cop busting drug lords
and pimps and saving her from the hopelessness of Oklahoma
and Reagan's trickle-down depression, for her resistance
to a place whose beauty lies in wheat fields and oil fields
and cattle fields and barren fields where nothing but mesquite
trees grow, whose beaches surround muddy lakes that'll stain
a white bathing suit faster than you can say *bleach*?
And how can you blame me for taking after my mother,
that bodily ache for things I can't possess—muscle cars
and Super Bowl tickets, Jennifer Beals dancing around my living
room in her *Flashdance* leotard? After all, there's an "I" in *family*
and another in *vice*, though it rides between two consonants
the way I'm sliding between the land of the living and the kingdom
of desire. Even now as I stand in my bedroom clutching
a honeymoon photo of me and my wife on a beach in Cozumel—
two lowercase i's wading in the surf beneath blue skies—
I'm thinking of someone else, a different wife, a better wife
standing on a better beach closer to Miami.

ODE TO THE MAN IN RED SWEATPANTS

When the man in red sweatpants on tonight's
episode of *COPS* says that, once finished
with a batch of kitchen sink meth, he boils
the coffee filters to siphon every last residual
molecule, I feel grateful to have my teeth intact,
to have sweatpants without any holes in them,
a house with houseplants and a decent back porch,
for I've been down, but not *that* down.
I've been low, but never *too* low, though I've
known folks who asked directions to the valley
of death, have talked to them during visiting hours,
wrote letters, sent care packages, and still I'm
grateful, as I imagine you are sometimes grateful,
that the man in red sweatpants is out there,
running around the woods, shirtless and dizzy,
trying to make things work or work things out
because somebody's gotta take one for the team,
someone has to be the goose among the ducks
at recess. While I was eating my unpronounceable
sandwich from the fancy sandwich place, the man
in red sweatpants was burning his fingers.
While you were busy blow-drying your hair,
the man in red sweatpants was keeping up
with demand for those of us hiding our lives
in plain sight like CIA operatives or that Boston
cream doughnut I didn't want my coworkers
to find among the glazed. Stand still and the beast
won't see you—or he will—in which case
your best defense is to run in circles, shouting

and thrashing your arms. Yesterday the news
reported that java stands in Seattle have turned
to sex to survive in the marketplace.
Picture light rain and scantily-dressed baristas
in black bras and see-through tops blowing
kisses, grinding beans, pouring steamed
milk from containers that, at certain angles,
reflect a distorted canvas of tan skin.
Picture the lady in Tulsa who got busted filming
love scenes with her lab and blue heeler,
my urologist advising me to drink more water,
masturbate less. And what about the man in red
sweatpants? Everything's going as planned until
the deputies escort him to the squad car.
He makes a beeline for the woods—a terrible path
to follow when evading law enforcement—
and gets tackled by Rosco, canine extraordinaire,
as the crowd goes wild. If the monkey doesn't get you,
the dogs will. If someone doesn't shoot you
in the face over car keys, you'll be struck
by lightning or die in a gas explosion. Have no fear.
Thy Fritos and bean dip will comfort thee.
Someone will prepare a table; heads shall be anointed.
These things will follow, will carry you until
every need's compressed, every drop squeezed
out like love, like the last sip of coffee
at the bottom of your cup.

SWIMMING THE ENGLISH CHANNEL

Midway through the fifth lap
and already I'm struggling to keep
my arms in sync, my body streamlined
to reduce drag. I've been coming
to the Y since May, but July's splashing
me in the face, saying it's time
to hang up my Speedos and call it a day.
But I like slipping into the heated pool
to revisit distant bathwaters and pretend
I'm swimming my own version of the English
Channel, just as I like praising the exactness
of models—the methodical calculations
and recalculations, the record keeping.
Besides, who's to say this cloudy tank's
not built to scale? The lifeguard twirls
a whistle around her finger, idly watching
the regulars—semi-retirees twice my age
who glide by with such fluidity
as to keep alive the fantasy that I, too,
may one day seem graceful,
that I could make the backstroke look easy
the way Tom Glavine makes a changeup
look effortless, a perfect bluff.
There are daydreams and then there are day-
dreams. Between sets, Dan, the 57-year-old
father of three, tells me swimming led him
to church, which led him back to the pool
like some circuitous baptism
and then invites me to Wednesday service.

I say *No thanks* and swim away in a kind
of half paddle, half breaststroke
because I don't believe things need saving,
but execution. I'm talking about
the leg bone connected to the hip bone.
I'm talking about movement
and endeavors of grand proportions—
grandmas running the Boston Marathon,
eccentrics swimming the Amazon,
mountaineers who climb Everest
despite frostbite and pulmonary edema,
hypoxia or the threat of losing
your fucking marbles in a land not suited
for the human foot when I can't even stand
chapped lips or the remnants of chlorine
rising out of my skin two days after a swim.
Still I come here, lest I succumb
to drowning, lest I hit bottom. You see,
I'm talking about heat exchange and objects
in motion remaining in motion.
I'm talking about channeling myself
toward something mystical and unimagined.
Something reckless.

ODE TO LOVE HANDLES

Pencil *You look like the Michelin Man*
onto a list of things not to say during sex,

as well as the ill-conceived reply that she is,
and always has been, a goddamn bore in the sack.

Understand when she confiscates your DQ Blizzard,
skims your milk, takes away your peanut butter

cookies, she wants you to grab a jog, eyeball
Oprah, comb *Men's Health* so you can solve

all of life's waddle problems. And, no, she won't
count *Playboy* articles as productive reading,

like the one explaining the best way to organize
a mini bar you quoted one night at a party

even though you've never owned a mini bar,
unless you count the kitchen cabinet with the half

bottle of Crown, plastic cups, birthday napkins,
and a blender you've used on two occasions.

You have to stand your ground. You have to say,
I will have potatoes mashed in gravy, spare ribs

and apple pie because I got a meat tooth
and a sweet tooth and room for all the sides.

When she pinches your *manos de amor*,
when she slaps your tummy and says you're

an image spit from your father—stretched at the lake
in his blue dolphin trunks, cold beer in one hand,

chicken leg in the other—you have to say,
I am the walrus, and I contain fucking multitudes.

Install handlebars if you want utility.
Ditch the spare tire if you want love without judgment.

And don't believe what they say, that women hold
on to them lovingly while you thrash around in the dark.

Know there are only so many ways to get from
point A to point B without extra baggage,

that none of us, no matter how round or monstrous
we become, can ever offer anything to hold.

LETTER FROM A HYPOCHONDRIAC

Dear Abby,
    Every day I wait for a phone call to tell me
a biopsy shows an army of malignant cells
standing at full attention. Often, *my* attention
turns to the pain in my right shoulder,
an old football injury I suffered during pregame
warm-up freshmen year. Any sensation of light-
headedness I may or may not be experiencing
encourages me to schedule another CAT scan,
an EKG, random blood tests.
    The doctors say I'm in perfect health.
They say my body clings to life despite myself.
But don't laugh. You know you've been there,
to the place in your life where every pain,
joint creak or unexplained tingling sends dread
tumbling to the bottommost compartment
of your bowels.
    When I thought I was going blind
due to migraines I suffered while reading Milton,
I consulted WebMD, which was not helpful,
then saw my ophthalmologist who, after two complete
exams, pronounced my eyes to be in working order.
He said I had 20/15 vision. He said I could fly fighter
jets á la *Top Gun*, all sharp turns and loose speed.
    My therapist says most people wait their
entire lives for something ugly to arrive in the mail.
I'm waiting for throat cancer, hip replacements,
some catch-all wasting disease that'll age me
like an old book. Sometimes I feel my prostate

enlarging like a diseased heart. Sometimes swells of bacteria eat through the halls of my brain until there's nothing left.

And Abby, when I hear the hazy breathing of my father spilling like water over flood gates, it is my breath, and I have to remember my lungs are fine. That I'm not about to drown.

UPON READING ELVIN JONES HAS DIED OF HEART FAILURE IN ENGLEWOOD, NJ

A week before you died
I listened to *A Love Supreme*
while changing the oil in my car
and felt that the way you played
was like the wind rolling across the plains—
sometimes a dust storm of heavy
grooves, sometimes the soft hush
of leaves on an August afternoon.

And now, after reading you died motionless
in a hospital bed, hooked to machines
and IV tubes because the chief organ
in your body responsible for rhythm
had given out, or given up, I think of all
the nights you must have been near
the end with the long solos under hot lights—
sweating so much you'd have to wring out
your suit. I think of the Vanguard, legato
phrasings, the track list enumerated
like a recipe for dying—*Acknowledgment,*
Resolution, Pursuance, Psalm.
Isn't that what we want our ashes to be,
a final song that hangs on the lips like salt,
the one hummed in the car, tapped-out
in your best shoes—*a love supreme,*
a love supreme . . .

POEM BEGINNING IN THE FRONT SEAT OF A CADILLAC

Early June and driving down a highway
with no idea where I'm going.

Like a giant, prehistoric bird
I feel the compass in my brain pulling

me across state lines toward some magnetic
destination I've only dreamed about.

My mouth is dry, but I can still taste
the coffee and jelly doughnut

I had for breakfast as I sit watching
a semi-truck burn to the ground

outside Monticello, Utah, a terrible place
with hideous rock formations

the color of antelope skin.
But I'm content to lean back and enjoy

the show. It is like a song, like the thing
I feel when the last of the evening light

seeps from the windows of my quiet house,
on my quiet street, and all that exists

is a stillness begging to be spoken to
or spoken for. I tell myself that it's only

light leaving a room, the way all
things must go, steady as the speed

of a second hand, a little less of her
in the bedroom, a little less of me

reflected in the bathroom mirror,
where each morning I deconstruct my face

with a razor and try to appear as something
more than a blur. Smoke rises

into the open sky. Far from the road,
two palominos feed on sagebrush.

OVERTIME

It's hard to make out my hands
    in the pale shop light. The sound of the grinder
against the rim accelerates to a sharp whine
    then steadies like a jet at cruising altitude.

I turn the wheel, grind, inspect, turn, grind
    watching sparks spread across
the cement floor. Lately, I feel like every day is a Tuesday.
    Right now, I feel like my skull's going to split
in two, as each second rust gives way to new steel.

Go outside for a smoke. A hawk wheels
    in the sky.

    There are things I wish I could talk about
with strangers. Tell them when I go, I hope to die inside
    a pecan grove or any stand of trees forming
parallel grids. I walk from one end of the shop to the other.
    It's like Saturdays at the zoo watching
the leopard pace from his feeding door to the last section
    of galvanized fencing.
He pivots his front-right paw in the same speck of dirt,
    working a permanent groove
into the ground.

I try to balance the tire—setting and resetting a piece
    of metal weighing no more than a few ounces—
all it takes to make the wheels on the bus go round,
    always and forever, as if everything is controlled
by some version of a tidal moon.

I'm always fighting my way out of something—
cramped cages, the sting of winter afternoons.
By day, jetways streak across the sky.
At night, red tower-lights signal in the east

until nothing is surprising anymore—
a woman's smile as she lets her hair tumble down
to her shoulders or a sudden flight of birds.

Here there is only the world and the wheel and a brief
colony of light.

SONG

The musky scent of pear blossoms
reminds me that soon the trees will leaf

out, and the marigolds I planted in the garden
will open sunward, and all will appear

to be falling into place. The dew catches light.
Birds call out to each other from across

the neighborhood. Faint glow in the window,
scent of red meat on a grill.

Because I don't know what it is to be the tree,
to feel the pulse of new leaves as a green

fire on my skin, I will go back inside,
pull down the shades, and try to dream up

a life that isn't so warm and bright,
as if sleeping could transform grief,

as if heat and a single blue arc could weld
the world back together.

Stag Night

We're drinking in a bar during the first hours
of a friend's bachelor party. He's drinking
some Scandinavian ale because he believes
light beer makes him skinny. Sometimes I'll buy
a 30-pack of Natural Light just to feel like
it's high school again, but tonight we need
something stout to meet here and talk and feign
interest in our lives. The waitress brings
buffalo wings smothered in ranch dressing.
Sometimes this is as good as it gets—fried chicken
and exaggerated claims from the past.
Dave remembers the half-torso our junior high
science teacher used to demonstrate the jigsaw
arrangement of our organs. She named the half-
torso Steve. Dave stole Steve's heart.
I took his left kidney. No one knows what happened
to his lungs, but I remember she told us a man
is the sum of his parts. Didn't someone say
things fall apart? Didn't three blind men fondle
an elephant and say the parts could never form
a whole? The bachelor starts to lose his shit
and flirts with the waitress who smiles and laughs
at his jokes though she looks as tired and bored
as those of us still sober enough to recognize pity.
At closing time, we drive back to our hotel suite.
Bottles are opened, joints passed around.
We all laugh when someone buys porn
on the TV. We laugh more when we hear
someone hired three strippers to come over

when they finish their shift at the club.
And when Candy, Genesis, and Starla arrive with impossible
names (though I once had a crush on a cheerleader
named Candy, who everyone said would put
out, but didn't), they're greeted with shouts
and dollar bills as they spin in and out of laps to Zeppelin,
and I think it's been a long time—*a lonely, lonely,*
lonely, lonely, lonely time since I paid for a dance
and felt how desperate each of us could be for
something new. One of the girls straddles me,
runs my hands through the crevice between her
breasts. Her skin is soft the way I imagine lily pads
would feel if I were silly enough to wade
into the middle of a pond to touch one.
The bachelor stuffs what's left of his money,
including a fifty, into his jeans, shouting
for the girls to come and get it.
Of course, he's too drunk to get it up and enjoy
what could be the high point of his life.
Sometimes this is as good as it gets, and nights
like these become the stuff of legend in the retelling
of the moment when the pants came off
and we all stared at something we've been afraid
to see—beer bellies and double chins, the flaccid
future dangling before our eyes. The girls' bouncer
says, that's enough. They collect their money
and leave. We go quiet like wildebeests in the presence
of a predator—lesbian nurses on the TV, Nine Inch
Nails on the stereo.

REUNIONS

This is the night of the living dead or the morning after,
which I always imagine as a hangover
of restless souls, human and zombie alike, converging
to maim each other in the spirit
of fellowship, but today we've come here for the brisket
and potato salad
and the moonshine, which threatens to melt the two-liter
Mountain Dew bottle into an emerald
puddle while a group of third cousins tune guitars,
fiddles, dobros, an electric bass,
before singing songs about the heartland and their collective
achy breaky hearts.
And so we'll huddle up because we are bound by blood,
or so the story goes. Year after year
we come here to catch up on the latest weather reports,
obituaries, the pitiful retelling
of Uncle Ed's death—a man who, as far as I can tell, was never
anybody's uncle—tales of triumphant
poker games or the purchasing of a new Lincoln, fables
with plots that remind me
of a pulp novel I once found at a truck stop in Tucumcari:
Trailer Park Trash,
a tale of two people whose "love was as mobile as their home."
Mobile love and mobile people
who once migrated from Mobile, Alabama to the southern
plains of Oklahoma
to work the oil fields and multiply, and now there are kids
running around the room I've never seen,
bodies floating to and fro inside the Seminole Convention

Center next to the Jimmy Austin
Golf Course where men in polo shirts are teeing off
on the eleventh hole,
dreaming of the nineteenth, bourbon and cigars for everyone,
while workers from the Department
of Corrections operate heavy machinery, pluck crab grass
from velvety greens.
What is this fascination with all the little cells of the world–
family reunions, class reunions,
Sting and The Police reuniting for one last performance
of "Roxanne"?
What is this love for folding chairs and vinyl tablecloths,
for supreme carrot cake,
for bullet holes and war stories, for rumors of illnesses,
stints in rehab,
for knowing at what age I can expect to develop Parkinson's?
The band revs up.
The music bears us as we bear the music, as we lay witness
to tradition and ceremony
and rituals, the way Cherokee women wear their hair long
until the death of a loved one,
then out come the scissors; the way small town citizenry
fill the stands on homecoming
adorned with war paint and gold bells; the way peaceniks
and students poured into Altamont
in '69 to watch Mick Jagger, all snarl and swagger,
sing "Gimme Shelter"
to a swirling mob of Hells Angels so they could feel like they
belonged to one great human tribe.
And I'll admit I'm partial to concerts and bikers
and leather jackets,

just as I'm partial to all these people who have my mother's
eyes and possess a genealogy
of patchwork quilts, some bearing the name of every first-born
son because we're a family
of male heirs, because we're phallocentric, because the band
plays on as I sit forking my carrot
cake and drinking my coffee before it goes cold, before I start
to forget the names.

SNAFU

Now that the day has been folded
and put back in the drawer and the streetlights
flicker with moths and the occasional bat,
I will put on my sneakers and take Max for his nightly walk.

We are like clockwork—little wheels for the turning,
      springs for the springing—
keeping ourselves leashed to a schedule
      as if commitment to order keeps the world
spinning on its imaginary axis.

Every morning I eat me Lucky Charms,
and every evening I watch TV while the sun drops
behind identical houses,

while shadows stretch across lawns
equally kept and tamed according to HOA regulations.

On Mondays I roll the garbage to the curb
and blow a kiss to the things I loved last week—
      pizza boxes and paper plates, uneaten apples
from the farmers' market.

Thank you beer for spilling your guts.
Thank you bulbs for the incandescent light.

Tuesdays I toss lawn darts.
      Wednesdays I pitch horseshoes.
            Thursday, Friday, happy days.

Saturday evenings my neighbors—three nursing students
splitting rent and house chores—jog down the street in ponytails

and black sports bras, keeping their own lurid schedule
but each listening to different music.

Inch by inch we learn that it is necessary
to walk upright no matter the toil,
to embrace bipedalness and shin splints
as we march our legs and pets under the orange,
    city-hazed sky.

~

The air is heavy with the smell of dryer
sheets and charcoal grills.

We pass kids playing basketball in the driveway,
the cracked and oil-stained court illuminated by security lights—
    dribble, pump-fake, jumpshot.

The tallest boy boxes out his opponents,

rebounds shots like Dennis Rodman, pre-tattoos
and NBA contracts, collecting college boards
    in Durant, Oklahoma.

He moves like my friend Colt back in high school,
driving the lane to the howls of the crowd,
bodies piling into a humid gym for the pregame gossip,
for flat sodas and popcorn, giant pickles and Pixy Stixs,

Colt's legs as pale and skinny as his namesake,
but moving with such balletic, dexterous speed
you had to stop and relish the sweet ambrosia,
the nectar of the moment between shot and swish.

I would live in that space if I could,
    caught between cause and effect,

the seconds before a raindrop hits the windshield,

just as my nephew would live inside a Chuck E.
Cheese's if you'd let him.

Yesterday he and I were good little rodents,
gnawing our way through waxy pizza and Dr. Pepper
before whacking moles with giant hammers,
shooting pixelated deer with imaginary rifles.

And when the fun was over and we were out
    of breath,

we picked through the spoils at the front counter–
    army battalions molded
from green plastic, airplanes carved from balsa
    wood–goods traded for tickets,
tickets earned with tokens, tokens we bought with cash–
    the market before the sugar crash.

I wanted to tell him this is how we transact our love,
our labor, that we are diminished by what endures–

animatronic circuits, rubber balls, cases of neon bracelets
whose atoms don't readily expire.

How do you explain why we don't glow in the dark
like the stars and planets above his bed?

How do you say we're a heap of ash, pile of bones,
enamel yielding to the acid of the years?

We are. We is. And *is* is everlasting.

~

This is not about nostalgia, but about beauty,
and if not beauty, then spring or wheat shoots
or Wall Street,

any of the vast and duplicitous sound bites that cycle
through our days—

sprinkled on the cereal, flavoring the coffee,
displayed in the headlines and Google searches
that infiltrate the minutes:

dirty jokes and unread emails, weed eaters and patio sets,
pop-ups that advertise breast implants, tooth whiteners,
Catholic School Girl Amputees,

streaming news bringing me the local and late breaking:
Nate Christian, 23, pleads guilty to breaking into The First Assembly
of God and using their phones to call sex hotlines.

What I know is that space is a vacuum.

What I know is this sky and its disappearance moves me a little,
a sudden drop in pressure, a catch in the throat.

~

Max pulls against me; he wants to stop reminiscing
and continue the walk. He wants better dog food, more bones.

He smells the rabbits that have invaded the neighborhood
like Normans, sacking flowerbeds and hobby gardens unmercifully.

One year field mice flooded our house, and I spent the summer
tossing glue-trapped bodies into buckets of water to drown.

Then rattlesnakes in the living room. Then hawks on the roof.

We pace ourselves in the cool air, peering into the glowing windows
at faces flickering in the LCD brightness or washing plates in the
    kitchen.
If it's dark enough, I'll watch them for a while and try to imagine
their ongoings, inhabit their bodies—watch what they're watching,
rinse what they're rinsing. I once saw a woman unsnapping her bra,
and she looked my direction, and I looked away.

You might say that is predatory, peeping tom-*ish*,
but I pledge we are better brethren for the looking.

If you ask me to housesit/babysit/dogsit, I will, dear friend,
despite conventions, pilfer through your drawers,

ransack your bedroom.
I will find your porn and dildos; I will spray your cologne,
thumb through your diary while wearing your house shoes.
And when you get home, I will act the same,
but love you deeper having smelled your dirty laundry,
having fingered your lingerie.

I feel Max's weight dragging against the leash
as we each visit the zoo of our desires.
On one hand, the taste for blood and cottontails.
On the other, the magnetic pull of wanting
to be somebody else.

But we walk on, and I scoop up his shit
with my plastic baggy hand,

and we go back home to roost, to wander, to lie in the hammock
on the back porch where it's bat-dark, nothing stirring, and watch
the radio tower lights flash above the rooftops,

amid the city lights reflected in the clouds
like a mirror fogged with steam.

I go inside and ask the missus for a glass of water,
for a meal ready to eat.

I meant to say something meaningful,
something verdant.

I wanted, for an instant, to say *Let me be your baby*
bird, your Western Sizzlin' Denver omelet.

~

I listen as the icemaker comes on, the hum of the AC,
the whir of the fan.

I think of Nate Christian waiting for his savior at the end
of a dial tone.

I think of a man licking the stump of a right leg
above which rests a plaid skirt with double-stitching,
wondering if there's something both exploitative
and loving in that caress.

Tomorrow I'll rise to make the bed
and clear the kitchen of coffee cups.

I'll rise to watch the air escape my lungs
before charting the values of 401(k)s and 403(b)s,
eavesdropping on client meetings where spouses
sit down over cookies and Diet Cokes, eager to plan
the next stage of their lives—the dream of retiring
in three years flat, of owning a villa in Tuscany
where their ancestors lived—and having those hopes
bulldozed by the bottom line:

You are the heap of ash, the pile of bones, oil rags
in the garage, spare change on top of the dresser.

You are. You is. And *is* is everything.

two

ODE TO SUEDE

I spilled my virginity on a suede sofa—*not* the luxurious
kind—the sort you buy on impulse at a discount outlet

south of town, upwind from a dog food plant.
This model came fully loaded with dark stains

and cigarette burns the size of rubies or the indentions
from a hole puncher. The couch had been stored

in my grandparents' avocado green camper trailer
ever since they purchased a new sectional with spring-

loaded footrests, pull-down armrests, and back cushions
so thick and fluffy they could make even the most portly

man feel at home. I watched Miranda undress down
to her socks. As our bodies moved against the fabric—

awkward at first, like an engine misfiring then starting,
then stopping and starting again—I could smell Old

Spice from the time my grandfather threw his spittoon
against the kitchen wall after losing four hundred

in dominos and had to spend the next three nights
curled like a fetus into the torn upholstery.

Miranda wasn't as sweet as her name, which I loved
because it rhymed with *veranda*—a sound like putting

pearls in my mouth, like brushing my teeth with caviar
at a time when everyone I knew sat on porches

built with cinder blocks and warped two-by-fours.
I didn't know what I felt then was not love,

not tenderness, but a rush of blood making me dizzy
and sick, though watching her—goosebumps on the skin,

nipples erect—I was ready to love anything. Afraid
I would come too soon, I traced my finger around the edge

of a burn mark, counting the revolutions in my head.
I thought of algebra and the chemical formula for bleach.

I thought about Andy's older brother Tom showing us
how he and his buddies played chicken, letting a Lucky

Strike burn to the filter on their forearms. When that didn't
work, I recited the names of fish I'd caught—*catfish, bluegill,*

sandies, striper, drum—and got lost in the naming like the day
loses its heat. The fear kept me moving. The suede made it soft.

THYROIDECTOMY

Once the woman is asleep, they tape her eyelids
and remove the top of her gown. Her large breasts
fall to the sides of her ribcage, and I'm a little

embarrassed to look there because I don't even
know her name. Fourteen years old, I'm watching
my surgeon-cousin Jim, who snuck me into the OR

because I want to be the next Doogie Howser,
pull this woman's throat apart like a puzzle
with a zipper. The lights in this place are almost

unbearable, as are the machines buzzing and beeping
and turning gears to maintain pressure and breath.
I ask, *Where's the epiglottis, where's the voice box*,

and then start to worry her stitches won't come out
right. *Scars don't become women*, my mother used to say,
and things aren't looking good for this patient

whose throat has become a honeycomb of broken
vessels while she lies there like a sheet on a clothesline,
only she's not swaying in some summer breeze,

but falling deeper and deeper into the steel table,
and then I remember my brother once clotheslined
me coming around the north corner of our house,

and I couldn’t talk for a week. The surgeons take turns
removing the gland in sections to check for signs of cancer
and calcium deposits, and I can’t stop thinking about scalpels

and recovery time, and how if she could sing from right here
on this very table, what would I hear with everything
pulled open like a piano full of mallets and wire and sound.

THE FIFTH OF JULY

Kids down the street pop leftover firecrackers,
and Max jumps from my lap, spilling Beefeater
down my shirt. For a second I want to kick him
or toss what's left of the ice and gin into his chocolate
face because I was taught that everything deserves
a little pain now and then. He comes back to the sofa,
ears folded back, looking culpable as dogs do
when they've disappointed their masters.
I say *Good boy* and roll his tennis ball across the floor.
Good boy for sitting, for fetching, for shaking
hands. I remember the summer I turned eleven–
Roman candles and cherry snow cones,
the smell of rust and old tires at the junkyard
where Tony and I dug through piles of scrap
for bicycle parts, cutting our hands on busted water
heaters, the doors from a once-green Chevelle,
and how the day after the *oohs* and *awws*,
the bombs bursting in air, we rode back to the park
to finish our pyrotechnics among the debris
of independence–beer cans and fruit rinds,
ashes from the bonfire scattered across the grass,
the whole scene like an actress thrust into daylight,
blemishes and all. We saw Spencer and his sister
twirling sparklers by the gazebo, the white light burning
like a welder's arc, and I thought of the time I watched
my father smelt a new hitch on Thurman's trailer,
and I stared into the blue light even though he told me
not to and had to spend the next day in bed with potato
wedges over my eyes. Spencer came over, all pleated

shorts and clean shoes. He bragged about his Rangers jersey,
his new bike, the handcuffs his parents bought him—
real handcuffs, a cop's handcuffs—the kind you could use
against resisting fathers or delinquent mothers.
The metal caught the sun like a prism as he latched
and unlatched each side, the beauty of new things
when everything we wanted had to be found, assembled,
or stolen from a pickup bed. The wind whipped up dust
and ash, and I looked at Tony just before he punched
Spencer in the eye, clenching his face into a tight ball
as he reached across his handlebars.
We could've stopped there, but because we were bored
or poor or too young to understand the particulars
of disappointment, we kicked him to the ground,
shackled his arms behind a lamp pole and tossed cherry
bombs at him in the heat—tiny explosions starbursting
whelps over his legs, his screams mixing with the pops
and bangs like an 8-track cassette. We stood there
and sweated fuses like cowboys timing their assault
on the unsuspecting stagecoach with a stick of dynamite—
jubilant, exalted, screaming into his wet face,
You crybaby! You fuckin' momma's boy!
What do you do when the day tries to burn out
your heart? How do you keep your hands steady
when the world gives you so much to cry about?
Years later Tony would drive me to a party in an empty
field below a planetarium of stars.
The goal was to shotgun a six-pack and run through
the darkness until you smashed into someone,
your atoms colliding with theirs. Much of me
is the same except I can afford better booze

and a little more light. In the morning I find the remains
of a possum Max has left next to my boots.
Such a sweet gesture. Such a good boy.
Some dogs never get used to the sound of gunfire
or fireworks. Some will break ice on ponds
just to retrieve what we kill.

THERE ARE WORSE THINGS I COULD DO

Sophomore year I got roped into running lights
and sound for my high school's production of *Grease*—
a fucking awful show that's only slightly more bearable
than *Oklahoma!* or *Miss Saigon*—by the vocal music teacher
who never liked me, who once gave me a week's worth
of detention for playing her piano, a woman who shall remain
nameless for it was I who egged her house that Halloween
and wrote *God hates you* in shaving cream. I took the job
because I was geeky and technical and believed in the power
of circuits and dials. My friend Dave ran the spots,
and when he'd drop the blue filter for Jennifer Murphy's
solo in "There Are Worse Things I Could Do," it was worth
sweating my balls off in the sound booth and the nights
I missed *Law & Order* just to hear her wail into the song.
On opening night, as mothers and fathers filed in to see
their babies dressed as greasers and tramps, remembering mid-
season that there's another sphere to the violence and blood
we love on the field, I was devoted, however hopeless,
to something I thought was bigger than myself—tweaking
the mics to the edge of feedback so her voice would swell
and rattle the walls of Elmer Graham Auditorium,
making us forget the humidity and empty storefronts along
Main Street. If you think this is sappy, it is. But what can I do?
Tear me open and you'll find organs approximating steel guitars,
bones reverberating in the past. There was a time when I held
some embryonic power in my cells like battery acid, charging
and discharging myself in the miracle of a keg stand.
But how quickly the checks bounce. In the most famous
of my grandfather's stories, he lifts a grown man off his boots

with a one-armed chokehold. Now there's not even a cool fire in his hands, just calcium and chewed wires. And what about Jennifer? We lost touch, having never said more than a passing hello, but I heard she's been losing electrons like the rest of us—stuck in a loop of laundry cycles and grocery runs with children hot-glued to her hips. Sometimes I think if the world had any justice, all our foolishness would be forgiven in the final scene as we're carried away in the seat of a Thunderbird.
It'd spit out something warmer than cold showers and TV dinners and droppin' pennies on a dream that won't come true.

PHOSPHORUS

The July heat rises like kettle steam into the open palm
of a treeless field. We moan and grunt as we heave

square bales onto the flat bed of a red Chevy–
my brother chewing a wad of Redman,

the black juice running off his chin, staining
his t-shirt. The smell of alfalfa is sickening

in the heat. The barn overflows with field mice–
easy prey for the owl who stares with eyes that shine

like dead obsidian from his perch on the back rafters.
Tonight we'll celebrate the end of a long, hot week,

piling into beat-up cars and dragging Main until
we're too shit-faced to see the truck in front of us.

After showers, we're cruising down Broadway in a haze
of tire smoke and aftershave, a case of beer

and enough soft packs of Marlboros to get us through the night.
In the distance the world is silent, but this street is alive

with the pale light of street lamps and the roar of stereos
as the air thickens with the smell of summer cooling

and the thought that somewhere, right now, a dog sleeps
under the carriage of his master's front porch,

a young couple is parked on the side of a county road,
a murder of stars above them like a black umbrella

in the sky, a late game home run rises into the bright heaven
of halogen lights, and you and I are crammed

into the cab of a red Chevy, windows rolled down,
burning like phosphorous, like celluloid.

GHOST OF A CHANCE

A man and a woman walk into a restaurant
off the main road. Blues plays in the background.

They take their time ordering but eventually
settle on the smoked trout and a bottle

of chardonnay. She wears a red dress,
one he hasn't seen before, and he is taken

by how good she looks. When the waitress
brings out the food, it's a long time

before he takes the first bite because the pink
fillet looks so artful in its yellow pool

of butter and garlic. Halfway through dinner
she lays her fork gently on the edge of her plate,

reaches across the table and holds out her hand.
He begins to take her hand in his, slowly

scrape his nails down her slender fingers
the way she likes when they are alone,

but stops. Beyond the flesh and bone of her hand
he imagines a miniature jazz band suspended

in her palm, playing accompaniment to the weary
resignation of Lester Young's solo in "Ghost

of a Chance." And for a moment he's sitting
in the nightclub of her palm, sipping scotch

and tapping his foot to the melody. Forgive
this man for his ambivalence, his numerous sins

of self-doubt and uncertainty. Forgive the words
he won't speak on the drive back to her apartment,

the failure and distance. But most of all, forgive
his blank stare and glassy eyes when the music starts up

and all he hears is the sound of his own heart and the slow
beat of an upright bass pounding inside his head.

B.A. IN ENGLISH

There was so much to learn in those days, so many
things I avoided by hitting the snooze button and counting
backwards from ten. I remember my first poetry professor,
an ex-chopper pilot who flew two tours in Nam before landing
on the conclusion that for all its Oxford-shirt dullness
academia is safer than bullets and leaky hydraulics,
and how one night over beers and corndogs he confessed
he's still terrified of trees except the ones that stand half-dead
and lonesome against the horizon like you'll see driving west
down I-40 toward Amarillo, where there's little more than clouds
and feedlots. This was at a time when I was really into hair gel
and The Pretenders and generally sabotaging myself,
be it sleeping with my girlfriend's sister or leaving the new
gallon of milk on the counter until things appeared in the jug.
I suppose reading the canon and getting high with Mike Chandler
between classes kept me sane, just as the adjunct professor
who complained about her band director husband and his boring
trumpet when she should've been dishing *Huck Finn*
and the transformative power of rafting, kept me entertained,
even if I wanted to tell her every Monday, Wednesday, Friday
to stick to the fucking text. What I remember most about that time
is not spiked hair, not Chrissie Hynde, not Huck and Jim counting
stars on the Mississippi or the nights I stumbled around campus
alone and drunk on Maker's Mark, but the semester I worked
nights in the adult GED program at Tomlinson Middle School,
where every evening I was paired with Frank, since I was new
and he habitually chewed the bones of his past, the ones you and I
keep buried in the yard, like how he'd sneak up close and talk
softly about shooting so much heroin he had to inject it in his cock,

the last usable vein in his body. These details clearly bothered
my coworker Sonja, who didn't care that Frank was a hardcore biker
until he revved himself into a coma after slamming his Harley
into the side of a minivan or that his brain had smashed against
the snow globe of his skull until families of neurons blew apart
and drifted down to the glittery street below. Now when he
carefully reads and pronounces *chilly*, he can't remember
if it means it's cold outside or that it's something you eat
when the weather turns blue. Once Sonja had had enough
of Frank's anecdotal life and told him to pack his shit and go home,
which he confused with *gnome*, and spent the rest of the night
convinced we were attacking the hat he wore to cover his scars.
At break I walked to the bench across the street where Sonja
and I met and smoked these skinny Croatian cigarettes her mother
mailed from back home. I told her any man willing to share something
about his dick besides size or splendor is legit, as in trustworthy,
but that only made me suspect as a fellow weirdo. Then I had to go
back inside and explain that spicy is not a designation of weather
but is relative to food, like *chilly* with an "i"— that it's all relative;
you could read Wordsworth or the back of a Kix cereal box
and find beauty and truth, or not, that we're all guilty of bait
and switch as we say one thing but mean something else entirely.
And I thought this would comfort Frank, as it did when I discovered
I could burn my girlfriend's toast or sleep with her sister
and the universe would judge me the same. But he just stared
into his workbook then looked at me and said, *The wreck decapitated
my girlfriend*, and I wanted to say, I know, Frank, but tomorrow's
a new day. The forecast said there's a chance the weather will be nice
and spicy, and if it's not, remember to hit the snooze button and count
backwards from ten, whispering, *There's no place like gnome.*

OCTOBER: a LETTER

Outside the day is full of tension, a kind of sadness
as autumn begins—nights getting cooler, apple trees swelling

with their last fruit, the smell of ash in the wind that reminds
me of the first girl I fell in love with and how one day,

after visiting her sick grandmother, the two of us walked
down a dirt road picking sunflowers

until we came to a bridge and made love there, in the cool
shade, shotgun shells and beer cans around our feet,

the sticky smell of weeds against our skin.
My dear, you are not that girl, though that's how I remember

it sometimes—you, leaning with me against the cold pillar,
your hands digging into the small of my back

while shadows move across a memory that is not needle sharp
and exact but long and broad like the stroke of a brush

whose beauty is matched only by its ability to bleed
moments and desires together, seamlessly,

until I'm not sure if it's dream or memory I'm longing after.
Outside the day is full of tension, a kind of sadness in early October.

PaRIS, tX

We move along at a certain velocity, a visible movement
through air as the speedometer vacillates between joy

and excess, hugging the shoulder, heading nowhere.
You might say *escape*. You might say *momentum*.

Just a century ago you and I were riding trains out into the prairie–
drifts of smoke, the hum of locomotive gears, and I wish

for all the salted peanuts of our days we could go back
to telling time by the pocket watch so I could smile and call

you Susan in the heat of 4:30. But time is now atomic;
a digital counter tracks electrons falling faintly

from a ball of gas, and we are here, half asleep, watching
the sun stretch across the flats of Texas because all we

have is the sweet nothing of the hour–bucket seats
and a radio instead of talk, a map in our hands showing us

the way east until we come to the next road sign:
Paris, 11 miles, so far from the dark Seine and artists

hawking portraits of the city's grand dame and her High
Gothic windows. This Paris, in all its lonestar glory,

boasts an Eiffel Tower topped with a red cowboy hat
as if to say, *We sell crepes during halftime*, as if to say,

Our distance is measured in yards. I've been told my lifeline
runs deep like an old river even though the channel

between my head and heart converges to a single yellow line.
It's the kind of road that gathers crows. This is the sort of town

that thrives on chinstraps and alma maters. What is driving
if not placing one foot in front of the other? What is a road trip

but sex with seatbelts and front crumple zones?
When the road turns to gravel, when the wheels let go,

give me bright lights and a scoreboard running low on time.
Give me a *Dead End*. Give me a *W*, give me an *I*, give me an *N*.

COMMUNION

Nothing ever tasted so strange as the air inside
the First Presbyterian Church on Kansas Street,
a mixture of wood polish and pastries.

At the beginning of service my brother and I
would grab the bell rope and pull against the weight
of oxidized iron that yanked us off our feet

with every pendulumatic arc, while the pastor—
whose only begotten son left the seminary
and drove west to become the next Brando—

led the congregation in hymn. I don't remember
the words they sang, but I can still see the blood-
colored glass and the wasps that buzzed

the sanctuary on Sundays in June.
Old pine and pastries. My brother used to drop
a handful of pennies into the plate and smile

while Mrs. Hart pressed organ pedals with bare feet
shrink-wrapped in pantyhose. I gave up the church
years ago, as did my parents who quit taking us

by the time I was smart-assing my way through seventh
grade. I don't know if it was busyness or laziness,
but we didn't even go at Easter—a clear violation

of the Bible Belt's mandatory spring observance
policy. These days I worship at the altar of easy joy—
the record player, the coffee maker, the truly immaculate

vending machine. Once my mother called to tell me
the fire department had been placed on call
because First Baptists were at that moment lighting

a bonfire to protest the hairless, washboard abs
and naughty girls with that just-caught-in-a-rainstorm
look packaged and sold by Abercrombie & Fitch—

deacons directing teens and tweens to toss their $80
jeans into the rising flames, while the youth ministry
blasted Christian rock anthems garnished with nose

rings and tattoos of the cross. *Isn't that nuts?*
my mother said. *At least it wasn't books.*
That night I dreamt of stonewashed denim curling

like Styrofoam plates, metal buttons glowing cherry
red in the embers. Some people want to be swallowed
by something holy, to fall into one dark tunnel after

another and still offer praise, ripe as a pomegranate,
to feel its texture in their mouths like pieces of flesh.
In our age of aromatherapy and self-help programs

teaching us to control the universe with our thoughts,
televangelists tell us god wants us to be rich, that our
futures are so bright we gotta wear shades.

Tell it to the preacher's dropout son, who got his big break
playing a cab driver in *Highlander 2: The Quickening*;
to the court clerk who shot her husband point-blank

in the face over an argument about predestination;
to the infant whose walker got stuck on the radiator
and for three days cooked like a glazed ham

because Mom and Dad had crashed from a crank binge.
Try as we might, we are not immortal like Christopher
Lambert or Sean Connery, though we like a bit

of swordplay now and then. The world breaks
with the burden of our burden as we learn that salvation
is a page in a coloring book wedged between pictures

of shepherds and sheep, Adam and Eve holding hands,
their bodies covered in leaves and earth, a giant,
ghostly-eyed whale swimming alone in the sea.

I don't say grace before dinner. I can't remember
the Lord's Prayer, but I've seen blood on the highway
and folks speaking in tongues. I know the flesh is flesh–

we disappoint ourselves. I know the Earth is a machine
grinding bone to dust, that my soul, if I have one,
must be stuck to the roof of my mouth.

tHREE

IF YOU AIN'T GOT THE DO RE MI

Someone in the hall yells *Dominoes!*
and just like that I'm shuffling bones
over a card table—the clink-clink sound
like dropping marbles into a wine glass.
Fresh coffee, a slice of pie, and all appears
as worn and smooth as an old Zippo.
We have a radio and a space to eat,
a space to talk, and when you don't
feel like speaking, a space for silence
and an ashtray or a game to pass the time.
I play the double six, sip my coffee,
and gaze into the faces of men who never
went to war, never fought for peace and love
or made it to college, but left the schoolyard
in the seventh grade and spent the last hours
of daylight welding horse trailers from the bare
bones of steel beams, oiled and smoothed,
then transformed into cages to haul
thoroughbreds to Shreveport, Santa Fe,
Oklahoma City, where four hooves
and a beating heart are the means
to a capital gain, a ticket for the small
things in life—new linoleum, new washer
and dryer, new teeth, the new smell
of a new car.

If I'm lucky, I'll lead this hand
with a dime or a nickel—anything
for a break, a good start. I take a bite
of pie. I run my thumb across the pips

on the tile as if reading the future in Braille,
picturing casinos off the interstate
shining like Vegas, Mecca of blinking
lights and three-dollar steaks, where before
there were only hay barns and unbroken
lengths of sky. I picture sparrows on a fence,
mockingbirds in the trees, farmers
planting subsidized corn in the dark
knowing it will fail, knowing if the roots
take hold they can fertilize every acre
until it burns and withers back into dust
for the coming spring—anything for a little
disaster relief, a handout in the heartland
because you can forget your stock portfolio,
forget about strapping what's left of your
belongings to a Model T and heading west.
There's no more California, no prospects
of fortune. This state's rush was in '68
when impulsive welders went north to work
the pipeline, sealing gaps with exquisite beads,
pretty as Victorian penmanship.

After all, this is where the wind
comes sweeping down the plains,
where license plates tell us everything is OK,
and it is, I suppose, so long as there's honey
in my honey bear and milk in the fridge.
For every gray sky, the kiss of spring.
For every dead field, rodeos in July—
the odor of cotton candy and horseshit,
popcorn and keg beer. We sit in the stands
waiting for a renegade bull or a clown

to get what's been coming for him
his whole life. Strange how much we love
disaster, how I'll watch the Daytona
500 hoping for a collision, praying for a spill,
until it's not so much a race as an assembly
of motorized billboards smashing into one
another at 188 miles per hour—100 more
than the 88 required to get back to the future
and away from clock towers and the pressure
to ensure your own existence.
    Someone changes the station and America
sings out on the radio—Crystal Gale followed
by Marty Robins followed by Woody Guthrie
and his tiresome locomotive blues—
song of the dust bowl, song of the banjo,
song of the boxcar and red clay dirt.
I check my watch. I drop a tile and look
for a pattern, though I've got nothing
but a double blank. I think I'm just better
on paper. There's more danger in a Popsicle
stick than my fingertips. The trick is to be
on the go, the way alcoholics' mouths
move even when they're not speaking.
On the muted TV they're showing images
of the Murrah Building—song of the Ryder
truck, song of ammonium nitrate.
The hours pile up like seeds in a grain elevator,
but if you got the money, honey, I got the time.
We start another round, draw another hand,
and I wonder about the places
I could've been tonight—song of Astroturf,

song of the reservation, song of the doublewide,
the La-Z-Boy, the microwavable pancake
dinner. The tiles start to resemble a jagged
spine misshapen after years of bad posture.
I try not to overthink the next play.
I tell myself that in the end every move's
the same, so you might as well take off
your coat and drop another quarter, say another
prayer, score the odds on horses and weather,
the likelihood of an early spring—
song of the cattle prod, the seed catalogue,
the convergence of pressure systems
that'll huff and puff and blow your house in.

Letter Sent Via Amniocentesis

Three weeks before your due date, and I can't stop thinking
of all the things I would revise if I, like you, were just stepping
into this world. For starters, I wouldn't have surrendered my bus
seat to Mickey Allen, the tallest and meanest boy in fifth grade.
I would have looked him square in the eye and thrown the meanest
left hook since Frazier. I would've learned to break-dance,
dated cheerleaders, stolen cars for the sheer thrill of getting caught.
You see, I'm talking now in the conditional tense—I would, I would not.
I would have never learned the intricate dance of apology and pardon.

There are many versions of your conception: Certain barriers broke,
other barriers did not exist. To this I've nothing significant to add,
but I will tell you that your father was young, though you will see
him age and crawl home stinking of grease. He was young and your
mother was young and I was young once, too, and soon you will
understand we come from a line of distant men who did not speak
or whistle while they worked, and one day you will also spawn
some version of yourself and learn not to recognize its presence.

You have to claw. You have to bite. You have to live without curfews
and anti-lock brakes because life can't be predicted no matter your
belief in horoscopes and crystal balls. Hold fast to the reins
because in all likelihood your parents will name you Lane,
after a deceased bull rider who was gored by the ugliest longhorn
in Texas, which means you're also destined to die at the hands
of something you love—cradled by that which punctures your heart.

You see, there is so much riding on you—the sins of your father
and your father's brother and a whole history of grandfathers stacked

like corpses atop your shadow's shadow. I am telling you this not so much for your own benefit, but for the memory of my past self still sobbing in the corner of some roller rink over the death of the mirror ball and young love. Hear me when I say this world is as bright as a coal mine, that you must use your hands or learn to see in the dark.

Phantom Pains

Morning and a pair of roses leaning against the lip
of a mason jar make me think of imaginary numbers
and the impermanence of organic compounds.
Like all of us, even newborns asleep behind panes
of plexiglass, the roses were dead the moment
they arrived. Now, staring at them from across the room,
I can see mold has gathered around the stems
turning the water a shade of green.
And so I tell myself this is how it should be—
a little rust bleeding into the stark, raw whiteness
of the petals, so I can once and for all quit believing
in longevity. In this equation, there is no interval
between possibility and a sure bet.
For my grandfather it was a question of artifacts,
collecting keychains and arrowheads the way children
are drawn to marbles and baseball cards.
I never asked him why, but I suspect it had something
to do with 1963, the year he lost his right hand to an oil
well and bad timing. He said he could still feel his fingers
in the form of a tightly clenched fist. I once watched
him scratch the end of his prosthetic hook while the radio
played songs about western heartache, songs with town
names like Midland and Bakersfield. All of this moves
in flashes like the light coming through the trees
while I sip coffee and read about how to winterize
a hot tub, a two-for-one coupon to the history museum
where they're showcasing a pioneer exhibit
complete with wax figures and the relics of nineteenth-
century life—six shooters and tobacco tins, hip waders,

shovels, pickaxes. In one room, wagon wheels and a set
of laudanum bottles. In the next, display cases
filled with handwritten ledgers kept by store merchants
to track what came in, what went out, like a narrative
of desire and acquisition. In this equation, let X equal
the momentary pleasure of sunlight, let Y equal
the sum of spoiled roses and nerves singing to things
no longer there. And I am grateful to have all my nerves
intact, save a botched wisdom tooth extraction.
But what is gratitude? What is wisdom? Most mornings
I lie in bed watching the gray light filter through Venetian
blinds and try to think of a reason to get up, get dressed
and face the day—coffee and Eggos and a cigarette
to ease my transition from one point to the next.
If I'm lucky, five o'clock will be here soon.
And then joy, and then the shock of joy,
and then nothing but the recollection of a feeling.

Into Soil

Where the green paint flakes from the hood and doors,
where daybreak illuminates the dirty streets,

where dogs no longer bark but lie quietly in the grass
the mystery ends and something like pain begins,

as the best of my intentions are lifted like fingerprints
from a wine glass, a smug kiss pressed upon the windshield

of a '53 Ford Victoria rusting against the fence line.
And the killdeer building its nest, and the mothers feeding

their young, and the sprinklers watering the lawns.
Can you hear it? Can you hear the static on the TV,

the rattle and hum of gunfire? Are you listening
from where you last left the lilacs blooming

in despair for a shooting star, for that western dream
some say still lingers over the dark, middleclass skies

of Ohio, Indiana, Missouri–Kansas, Oklahoma,
Texas? Nerves singing. Bodies singing as the heart

erodes into soil, as the river rises then departs like steam,
like mist in the woods where moss grows thick among

the detritus and tall pines that rise sixty feet
before branching toward the bright decaying stars.

HYMN

The wrought-iron fence, decorative
metalwork intertwined with white roses,
is alive with the hum of summer bees.

Inside, Quaker pews face one another
like tapestries on opposite ends
of a home, and the hardwood floor,
heavy with the smell of varnish and pine,
shines in the light pouring through gothic
windows. No one speaks.

The idea, I'm told by the friend
who brought me here, is to observe
silence. It is so quiet I can hear
the slow breathing of the woman
sitting next to me, who smells of lavender oil.

An hour into service a middle-aged man
stands up and begins talking
about his dead wife, her seven-year
battle with cancer, how he felt when he flung
her ashes into the Potomac on a gray afternoon
last February. No one replies. A few nod,
but most look out the windows or carefully
unwrap peppermints—there is no sermon.

They say silence gives meaning to sound,
that if you're quiet long enough the world
becomes apparent and you can hear

everything—cancer cells and worker bees,
river water and the sound of iron rods
being hammered and welded into something
beautiful for the climbing rose to cling to and die.

STILL LIFE WITH POMEGRANATES

Three pomegranates resting in a porcelain bowl
atop a worn oak table. The light in the window
suggests autumn, and you can sense that leaves
have gathered outside the kitchen door,
a dead hen hangs from the rafters waiting
to be plucked and boiled for soup.
The painter shows only the necessary details,
as he must have worked into the early hours
to guide our eyes toward the simple pleasure
of three red spheres lying in a cracked bowl.
He doesn't suggest it was the pomegranate
that tempted Persephone underground,
or that certain Roman-era coins depicted Aphrodite,
the goddess of abundance, holding the fruit in her
upturned palm, nor does he allude to Botticelli's
infant Jesus clutching what appears to be
a human heart torn down the middle.
The painting gives so little, and I ask for more—
whitewashed plaster and wood smoke, a pair
of muddy boots by the door. I want hunger spread
over the canvas with a pot of steaming soup
and a sharpened knife, the hands of a woman tearing
into the fruit to get at what matters inside.

COLOR DEPICTING THE INHERENT VALUE OF THINGS

White blooms in the trees
give shape to the dark street below.

Everything we know, a contrast—
the muted female cardinal,

black and white photos, conflicting
blots of color on canvas.

And we are no different,
painting every wall,

every surface down to the kitchen
ceiling. Call it a fresh start,

a new place where the body
can grow, the relationship

between crab and shell.
So many hues, so much confusion

mixed into every gallon,
but if we can believe in the palette

and the wheel, complementary
shades dividing the bedroom,

we can believe in anything.
Because I am terrible with my hands,

entire systems fall away from me—
brush patterns and engine mechanics,

the finer points of operating
a table saw. But she leaves nothing behind—

no separations, no bleed through,
no holes in the fabric of the spell

we're under—*Plum Rose, Island*
Green, Desert Sand. Her hands

are as magnificent as the night
she rolled three joints for me

and my two roommates
when we had nothing but time

and the starless blue horizon—
not sky blue, but the electric

blue flame on a grill.
Everything we know, a contrast,

another division of color—
ivory bones, pink lungs, gray feathers

bleeding into the worn-out red
of old barn doors, thunderheads

swelling behind the last bits
of sun. Buy me a house I can arrange

and mold into something elegant.
Hold me to every square foot,

every habitable corner—red bricks,
white door, nice even coats of paint.

HOLLOW LIGHT

Tonight I walked into the yard,
still dizzy from the wine at dinner,
and stood smiling at the January
moon, incandescent and blue.

In winter nothing is usable.
Everything is there for the viewing—
even breath has form.
It's the ultimate look-don't-touch
store full of china, and every glass
branch, icy and radiant, stands
still as the moon seeps over the plains
with its relentless hollow light.

So different from the candy pink
mimosa blossoms and the gold
summer wheat, tonight the stars
are fixed high and wide,
and below them fields of winter
grass shine in the bitter air
with the hard glint of crystal.

ELEGY FOR WHAT CAN'T BE SAID

This room, this bed of clean sheets, lilies sprigged with cut lavender
on the nightstand, is not an elegy. This song is.

There are days when we walk wires of grief and convince
ourselves to hold on—knuckles white, fingers worn to bone.

And then there are times I have to refrain from kissing you so hard
it would threaten death by drowning. You and I have never

known grace no matter how hard we've tried graceful acts.
You cannot conjure elegance—I learned this slowly—

it is not a summoning act. It is only a prayer, another selfish wish
on a star in winter. The spark we have is contradiction and perseverance

and maybe a little fear. *Fear*, not the kind you find inside a dark,
unfamiliar room but the lump on a woman's breast

that may or may not be benign. Today, while the sun rose
above hay fields heavy with fog,

I watched two rabbits eat the tomato vines you planted
last spring. I thought, *consciousness in action*, but that's too formal.

It's tough juggling between the wanting you and the not wanting you,
tougher still waiting for shutters to be flung open,

playing out days of words and doubt, wondering if the next moment,
the next day or week will open

some tucked-away truth if I can only speak loud enough to hear—
Say it, say it, I have said.

Flash Point

Four-thirty in the afternoon. The worst time of day by many standards—
traffic jams, sunlight glaring through the windshield all sharp
and one-sided like a bad argument. The woman ahead of me
in line at the hardware store looks frantic as she pays
for six garden hoses, fumbling with her billfold and saying
something about having to soak everything down.
After months of drought and high winds, wild fires have swept
the countryside with news reports of entire counties burning
and farmers being driven to near extinction, and suddenly
I feel silly holding a bottle of wood glue and a Dr. Pepper,
preparing to mend a couple of broken chair legs, while this lady
is worried about heat and embers and driving the fifteen miles
out of town to where the latest flares have risen near her home.
Tragedy & Comedy: The two faces hung on the right side
of my sister's vanity to remind us that, contrary to the Fig Newton,
life is not always fruit and cake, that there's only so much Mr. T
and the A-Team can do before the plot wears thin and you're left
with the empty feeling that heroism and noble mercenary work
are dead. And so as I'm gluing the last chair leg, I say to myself,
Let it all burn down, the whole damn state of affairs, like the time
I burned the woodpile next to my neighbor's shop,
and not even the heap of ash or the sheet metal, which buckled
under the heat, could satisfy my hunger. I wanted to see the whole
mess fall—the shop, the house, every last blade of grass.

FEEDBACK LOOP FOR THE APOCALYPSE

Pain comes from the darkness
and we call it wisdom. It is pain.
—Randell Jarrell

The end of the world is scheduled for next week.
I have seen visions of fire in the news—
hurricanes and peak oil, films about dolphin slaughter
and fishies in the ocean disappearing from the scene.

I have seen visions of fire in the news—
bees collapsing, polar bears drowning,
fishies in the ocean disappearing from the scene.
The tarp on my neighbor's grill balloons in the wind.

Bees collapsing. Polar bears drowning.
Turn on the TV there's more bad news.
The tarp on my neighbor's grill balloons in the wind,
making the sound of a sail whomping on the sea.

Turn on the TV, there's *more* bad news.
As I'm watching, there's pain in my right testicle
making the sound of a sail whomping on the sea
because I have a cyst or an infection or cancer.

As I'm watching, there's pain in my right testicle.
The sonogram looked like a malleated dolphin's skull
because I have a cyst or an infection or cancer
depending on which doctor I see.

The sonogram looked like a malleated dolphin's skull.
I showed my neighbor Alex, who loves *Flipper* reruns,
and asked for his independent diagnosis. He agreed.
On TV, *Flipper* jumps through a hoop then saves a family.

I showed my neighbor Alex, who loves *Flipper* reruns.
He doesn't know he'll grow up and train them for our delight,
teaching Flipper to jump through hoops and save lives alike.
He's such a lover, you will discover, when he steals your heart.

He doesn't know he'll grow up and train them for our delight,
then turn activist and free them from the nets of Japanese fishermen.
He's such a lover, you will discover, when he steals your heart.
The child is the father of the dolphin and so must come full circle.

Turn activist and free them from the nets of Japanese fishermen?
Nah. I like eating tuna salad and sushi too much.
The child is the father of the dolphin and so must come full circle?
You can't make a seafood omelet without breaking a few dolphins.

I love eating tuna salad and sushi, maybe a little too much.
I like squeezing lemon over a piece of meat red as a shade of lipstick
and eating dolphin omelets in my quest to be a yuppie.
There's nothing warm Saki and egg-drop soup won't fix.

I like squeezing lemon over a piece of meat red as a shade of lipstick.
The movie shows a harpoon being driven into a dolphin's skull;
I think there's nothing warm Saki and egg-drop soup won't fix.
The networks will broadcast this over and over until you puke.

The movie shows a harpoon being driven into a dolphin's skull–
blood churning in the wine-dark sea.
The networks will broadcast this over and over until you puke,
like a Michael Jackson primetime special.

Blood churning in the wine-dark sea.
I feel like a clubbed seal pup, skinned and deep-fried,
having watched the Michael Jackson primetime special
three nights in a row.

I feel like a seal pup, clubbed and skinned alive,
worrying about mercury levels and Alex eating his Filet-O-Fish
three nights in a row.
I once held a thermometer to a lamp until it exploded.

Worrying about mercury levels and Alex's Filet-O-Fish,
I caution him not to swirl quicksilver with his fingers,
recount the time I held a thermometer to a lamp until it exploded,
believing I could control anything.

I caution him not to swirl quicksilver with his fingers.
I say, our ancestors made flutes from swan bones,
believing they could control anything–
Ahab tossing his pipe, thumping his whale-leg against the quarter-deck.

I say our ancestors made flutes from swan bones,
lit their homes with ambergris.
Ahab tossed his pipe, thumped his whale-leg against the quarter-deck.
I say, soon we will make mud huts

and light them with bacon grease.
We will witness hurricanes and peak oil—
huddled in mud huts carving dolphins out of chair legs.
The end of the world, dear boy, is scheduled for next week.

SHRAPNEL

Last week I heard that a guy I used to work
with at a record store was killed somewhere

in the Anbar province (Arabic meaning *ware
house*) when an I.E.D. dismantled his right leg.

The portrait of his face as I remember it blisters,
and I often wonder if he died instantly or several days

later as his body turned pale and septic, while school
buses back home were busy loading children

from the sidewalks, and sprinklers watered the great
lawns of suburbia. Already the morning is humid

and full of bird song, but I don't want to think *song*
or *lullaby*. The absence of sound is a blade that cuts

closer to bone until the world is reduced to its basic
intentions–hunger and parallel lines, death and disease.

A woman I once knew told me she loved the smell
of silage and the patchwork canvas of Holsteins

on her father's farm. She said as a young girl her body
would disappear into the shrill droning of cicadas

at dusk. It was not the sound itself she loved,
but the bitter appetite, the suicidal lust for oblivion

that echoed from pecan trees along the creek.
The call filled the spaces of her body,

and as summer changed into autumn, she swore
she could hear them dying. The airless morning

swells after weeks without rain. It is something,
I think, to be entirely occupied with the living.

ELEGY WITH A BALCONY AND OPENING CREDITS

Tonight I am small. I contain solitudes, similitudes
of a life I once raised a glass to while observing a stalk
of summer wheat, but here in the Palace Theatre,
watching the *Die Hard* double feature, I've got it all—
popcorn and diet soda, coming attractions with vampires
and robots, built fast for those with ADD, and I think if you'd
wink at me, flash a little preview of what's to come,
then maybe later we could bring two sticks together
and catch fire or at least make a spark. Sometimes we're kindling,
sometimes the ash, but when McClane starts kicking ass
I feel alive and cavalier until he runs across broken glass,
and I reach back to touch the thin spot in my hair,
knowing you feel embarrassed for bald men the way I felt
embarrassed in the Wal-Mart bathroom for the paraplegic
emptying his catheter into the floor drain, caught like a cricket
in a web in the middle of the room. O the entanglements
we fly into and must escape from by coming to a place with dirty
ceilings and sticky floors, a balcony on the edge of collapse.
And so I'll toast to the season, and to the self, and to the thunderstorm
that churned above the library where yesterday I checked out
Barry Switzer's autobiography and found, buried between recruiting
violations and wishbone formations, a bookmark illustrated
with cartoonish kids riding mountain bikes toward the sunset,
as in *Look, ma, no hands!*, as in the transformative power
of reading. On the back someone wrote *Fuck books* in magic
marker. I laughed, then thought about regret and the improbability
of time travel because I'd repeat the second grade just to write
something as mean and direct on the bookmarks I kept next to the glue.

Instead of Be mine on the Valentines, I'd chisel a new gospel
in capital red letters—*I don't like you. You're ugly. The Magic Eight Ball says you'll be single and pregnant by junior year.*
O the things we wish to revise, the ways we wanted to change.
I'm disappointed no one mentions the positive side of Jeff Goldblum's
character morphing into an insect-human hybrid in Cronenberg's
1986 remake of *The Fly*. Sure he develops sores and must vomit
on his food before ingesting it, and, yes, he wrecks his relationship
with the attractive Geena Davis character, but what people forget
is simple conversion. Seth Brundle steps into one telepod and emerges
from another, stronger and unique. I had acne in high school.
I dated a girl who threw-up her food *after* ingesting it, but we
didn't change into the things we wanted to be—the bluebird, dolphin,
or tiger. I wanted to be the spider, the fiddleback making you dosey
doe with my toxic song. Besides, who needs books when I've got
Bruce Willis hissing *Yippie-ki-yay motherfucker!* and tossing bad
guys out of thirty-story windows? Who needs imagination
when I've got De Niro talking to himself in the mirror, Glenn Close
boiling bunnies on the stove? Watch something long enough and you'll
love it a little. After surgeons tore apart my shoulder, I spent the next
day watching a *Columbo* marathon on a 14-inch screen, and now I've got
a soft spot for Peter Falk's glass eye, just as I must cite John Wayne
as an early influence because Moms made me watch reruns of *Rio Bravo*
in lieu of a father. *Ya need to man up, pilgrim!* The second feature rolls,
and Bruce is back, all shaved head and designer leather jacket, living free
and dying hard as he combats terrorists and hackers in CGI. And when
the moment comes for the catchphrase that'll make the implausible
disappear, the last word gets drowned out by the sound of something
exploding. I weep and throw a handful of Junior Mints at the screen.
Sometimes you're the accelerant, sometimes the charred meat
at the bottom of the grill. But maybe if I run my hand up your skirt,

remembering how your Nazarene father banned you from tank tops
and matinées because he knew what can happen in the dark,
then maybe we'll be forgiven, and I'll whisper, *Are you the gatekeeper?*
And you'll say, *Are you the keymaster?* The movie is almost over,
and Bruce is out of bullets. Soon houselights and ending credits.
Soon the evening will call us home, and we'll be forced to live another
day, so let's call in sick and stay for another reel the way I used to fake
fevers to watch *The Neverending Story* and learn every minute how
The Nothing surrounds us. Let us break up the seats and make shelter.
Let us fall to our knees and worship the projector. May our teeth be
pulled to the sweetness of a cavity, our days be royal and easy, screened
in silver, a motion picture, while usher-boys wait to sweep the palace.

acknowledgments

Thank you to the editors and staff of the following journals, in which some of these poems first appeared:

Big Muddy: "Phosphorus," "There Are Worse Things I Could Do," "Feedback Loop for the Apocalypse"
BLIP (formerly *Mississippi Review Online*): "Elegy with a Balcony and Opening Credits"
Cimarron Review: "Lessons in Childhood Development," "The Fifth of July"
Copper Nickel: "Reunions"
Gulf Stream: "Thyroidectomy"
H_NGM_N: "Phantom Pains," "Color Depicting the Inherent Value of Things," "Stag Night"
Harpur Palate: "If You Ain't Got The Do Re Mi"
The Louisville Review: "Into Soil"
Lumina: "Still Life with Pomegranates"
Main Street Rag: "Paris, TX"
Nimrod: "Hymn," "Miami, OK," "Shrapnel"
Oklahoma Today Magazine: "Hollow Light"
Pebble Lake Review: "Upon Reading Elvin Jones has Died of Heart Failure in Englewood, New Jersey," "Morning Prayer," "October"
The Pinch: "Swimming the English Channel"
Poet Lore: "Ghost of a Chance"
Prairie Schooner: "B.A. in English," "Ode to the Man in Red Sweatpants"

I am grateful to so many who supported me while writing this book including Chelsey Simpson, Daniel Long, Jeff & Sandy Simpson, Jason Roberts, Clay Matthews, Labecca Jones, Brian Gebhart,

Robin Carstensen, Scott Norenberg, Dinah Cox, Adam Wright, Peter Lyon, Matt White, Tricia Damron, Matt Burch, Annie & Heath Whitfield, my lunchtime audience at OAEC, and the faculty and staff at Oklahoma State University.

Thank you to Lisa Lewis for her guidance, support, and immense generosity.

Thank you to Campbell McGrath for his kind words.

Thank you to Tom C. Hunley and Steel Toe Books. I couldn't have done this without you.

And especially to my family—you know who you are.

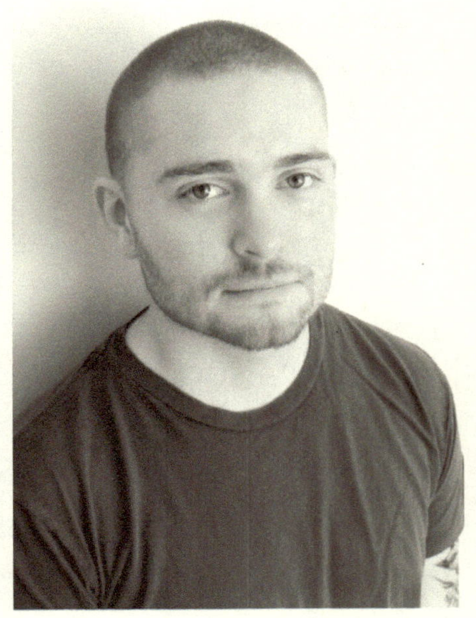

JEFF SIMPSON was born and raised in southwest Oklahoma and received his MFA from Oklahoma State University. In 2010 he was selected as a finalist for The National Poetry Series. His poems have appeared in *Prairie Schooner, Cimarron Review, BLIP, Copper Nickel, Harpur Palate, Poet Lore, H_NGM_N,* and elsewhere. He is also the founding editor of *The Fiddleback*, an online arts & literature journal. Visit him at www.jeffsimpson.org.

www.ingramcontent.com/pod-product-compliance
Lightning Source LLC
LaVergne TN
LVHW050934080826
845145LV00004B/1254

* 9 7 8 0 9 8 2 4 1 6 9 5 2 *